THE BAUHAUS PROJECT III: BERLIN

Tom Jacobson

BROADWAY PLAY PUBLISHING INC
New York
www.broadwayplaypublishing.com
info@broadwayplaypublishing.com

Cover photo by Francisco Hermosillo III

First edition: December 2024
I S B N: 979-8-88856-038-9

Book design: Marie Donovan
Page make-up: Adobe InDesign
Typeface: Palatino

THE BAUHAUS PROJECT III: BERLIN had its world premiere on 20 July 2024 at Open Fist Theatre Company in Los Angeles (Producers Martha Demson and Amanda Weier, Associate Producer Nychelle Hawk). The cast and creative contributors were:

OWEN...Jack Goldwait
ELLIS ....Katarina Joy Lopez
KAI ....John C Sweet
DUCK .... Sang Kim
BREC.. Chloe Madriaga

Director.. Martha Demson
Assistant Director... Sarah Zuk
Stage Manager ....John Dimitri
Set design .... Richard Hoover
Lighting design .... Gavan Wyrick
Composer & sound design .... Tim Labor
Costume design..Michael Mullen
Prop design ....Bruce Dickinson, Ina Shumaker
Projection design...Gabrieal Griego

CHARACTERS

ELLIS, *20s-30s, theatre student, Southern accent, also plays:*
    FRITZ ERTL, *30s, architect, carries a red book with a white spine*
    OTTI BERGER, *30s, textile instructor, Jewish*
    ADOLF HITLER, *40s, Chancellor of Germany*
    ALMA MAHLER, *72, composer and doyenne*

BREC, *20s-30s, graphic design student, from Los Angeles, also plays:*
    LUDWIG MIES VAN DER ROHE, *40s, architect*
    MARIA KIPP, *51, textile designer*

KAI, *20s-30s, fine art student, from New York, also plays:*
    ALFRED ROSENBERG, *40, National Socialist philosopher*
    GESTAPO OFFICER
    LUDWIG HILBERSEIMER, *48, architect and instructor*
    ARNOLD SCHÖNBERG, *76, composer, Viennese accent, smokes*

OWEN, *20s-30s, environmental design student, English accent, also plays:*
    RUDOLPH DIELS, *33, Gestapo Chief*
    WALTER GROPIUS, *50 and 68, architect*

DUCK, *20s-30s, ESL music student, strong accent, also plays:*
    WASSILY KANDINSKY, *66, painter, Russian accent*
    BAUHAUS STUDENT
    ZENOBIO REMEDIOS, *47, textile studio manager*

SETTING

The action takes place in an art school in Southern California in the present, in the Bauhaus in Berlin, Germany in 1933, and in Los Angeles in 1951.

SPECIAL THANKS

Josh Adams, Cyrus Alexander, Jonathan Bangs, Colin Bates, Bryan Bertone, Lou Danziger, Fran de Leon, Martha Demson, Presciliana Esperolini, Amanda Fekety, Éva Forgács, James Fowler, Ramón Garcia, Nychelle Hawk, Sarah Hollis, Jully Lee, Chelsea Kurtz, West Liang, Ramone Muñoz, Gary Patent, Kacie Rogers, Isabella Roland, David Shofner, Peter James Smith, Michael Sturgis, Donathan Walters and Dylan Wittrock

(An ugly black space. Pre-show: In the lobby stands a large sculpture composed entirely of modernist detritus. KAI, the artist who created this piece of rhyparography, stands next to the piece, silent unless spoken to, but secretly eager to explain the art. Signage indicates it's for sale. Inside the theatre, four 21st-century STUDENTS [OWEN, BREC, ELLIS and DUCK] situate themselves in chairs around the edge of the stage and get into costume [costume changes are generally in view of the audience throughout the performance]. Just before the play begins, KAI joins them. When they are ready, a title is projected in Bauhaus font: Berlin, February 1933. Two of the STUDENTS come forward in 1933 attire: BREC AS MIES VAN DER ROHE wears an elegant long dark coat, carries architectural plans and escorts OWEN AS GROPIUS, who wears a hat.)

OWEN AS GROPIUS: *(Looking around, fingers to temples)* This is awful.

BREC AS MIES VAN DER ROHE: *(Cheerful bass voice, hands on hips)* Of course. It's an abandoned telephone factory.

OWEN AS GROPIUS: Our buildings in Dessau—!

BREC AS MIES VAN DER ROHE: Beautiful. I miss them, too, Walter.

(Behind them, ELLIS AS BERGER, KAI AS STUDENT and DUCK AS KANDINSKY begin transforming the space, slowly turning black to white.)

OWEN AS GROPIUS: The Dessau Town Council wants to tear the Bauhaus down!

BREC AS MIES VAN DER ROHE: Unlikely. But almost amusing in a grim way. Look what the *Anhalter Tagezeitung* says about it.

(BREC AS MIES VAN DER ROHE *gives* OWEN AS GROPIUS *a newspaper clipping.)*

OWEN AS GROPIUS: *(Reads)* The banishment of this supposed "institute of design" will mean the banishment from Dessau of Jewish-Marxist "art". One can only hope complete destruction follows, this severe glass aquarium of oriental taste replaced with traditional homes and natural parks for healthy German living.

BREC AS MIES VAN DER ROHE: The provincials can't reach us here in Berlin.

OWEN AS GROPIUS: Who's paying for this, Mies?

BREC AS MIES VAN DER ROHE: I am.

OWEN AS GROPIUS: No government sponsor?

BREC AS MIES VAN DER ROHE: I've paid twenty-seven thousand marks over three years for this—

OWEN AS GROPIUS: Horror.

BREC AS MIES VAN DER ROHE: Already we're turning it into the Bauhaus. White walls!

OWEN AS GROPIUS: You can't even see the school from the street! That rickety fence! It's practically hidden!

BREC AS MIES VAN DER ROHE: An advantage these days. *(Pause)* You're appalled.

(OWEN AS GROPIUS *gives a pained smile.)*

BREC AS MIES VAN DER ROHE: Bauhaus Dessau rose from the ashes of Bauhaus Weimar, an eternal phoenix.

OWEN AS GROPIUS: Misunderstood again and again—

BREC AS MIES VAN DER ROHE: Your vision's rising once again in Berlin.

OWEN AS GROPIUS: Thank you. I know it's been at great personal cost—

BREC AS MIES VAN DER ROHE: Definitely worth the twenty-seven thousand—

OWEN AS GROPIUS: Spiritual, not just monetary. Is it true you let Gunta go?

BREC AS MIES VAN DER ROHE: She resigned.

OWEN AS GROPIUS: But—

BREC AS MIES VAN DER ROHE: I asked her to, yes, under great pressure from the reactionary students and the Dessau government. A mistake I'll not repeat.

OWEN AS GROPIUS: She says it was her or the Bauhaus itself.

BREC AS MIES VAN DER ROHE: I hope our survival proves worthy of her sacrifice. That's why I'm determined to keep the school going.

OWEN AS GROPIUS: But do you have students?

BREC AS MIES VAN DER ROHE: Many followed from Dessau and we get new ones every day.

(DUCK AS KANDINSKY *appears, sporting a cardigan and ramrod posture.*)

DUCK AS KANDINSKY: *(Russian accent)* Gropius! Welcome to the Bauhaus!

(DUCK AS KANDINSKY *hugs* OWEN AS GROPIUS)

OWEN AS GROPIUS: Kandinsky! How is Nina?

DUCK AS KANDINSKY: Happy to be out of wilderness of Dessau! See around you beauty and sophistication of Berlin!

BREC AS MIES VAN DER ROHE: Tell Walter about your classes—excellent students—

DUCK AS KANDINSKY: Class. Singular. Only one this term. Reduced hours, reduced pay—

BREC AS MIES VAN DER ROHE: We're just re-establishing ourselves—

DUCK AS KANDINSKY: Nina is very—how you say?—*slender* this days!

OWEN AS GROPIUS: At least you have a position, Wassily! Painters in Germany now—

DUCK AS KANDINSKY: Grateful I am for scraps.

(*Off* BREC AS MIES VAN DER ROHE'S *look*)

DUCK AS KANDINSKY: I am joke with you, Mies! Excuse, please. I go paint toilet now.

(*As* DUCK AS KANDINSKY *leaves:*)

BREC AS MIES VAN DER ROHE: He's not joking.

(*Although only a portion of the black has turned white, it already looks much better, and the* STUDENTS *hang party decorations and elegantly drape the walls.*)

OWEN AS GROPIUS: Kandinsky looks out for Kandinsky. Mies, do you need money? I've got a little—

BREC AS MIES VAN DER ROHE: I'll keep your dream alive without your money, my friend.

ELLIS AS BERGER: (*Appearing, wears a cloche hat*) Herr Gropius!

OWEN AS GROPIUS: Otti Berger! I thought you left the Bauhaus!

ELLIS AS BERGER: I have my own weaving studio here in Charlottenberg, but Hilberseimer drafted me to help tonight.

OWEN AS GROPIUS: Tonight?

ELLIS AS BERGER: It's Mardi Gras! We've only just arrived in Berlin and we're having a party!

OWEN AS GROPIUS: *(Laughing)* That's so Bauhaus.

BREC AS MIES VAN DER ROHE: A fundraising party.

OWEN AS GROPIUS: In that case, permit me to contribute!

BREC AS MIES VAN DER ROHE: Put your money away!

ELLIS AS BERGER: Perhaps you'll donate a rendering for our silent auction.

OWEN AS GROPIUS: Who'd bid on that?

ELLIS AS BERGER: Fans of Sommerfeld House, Torten estates—

OWEN AS GROPIUS: I don't have fans!

BREC AS MIES VAN DER ROHE: If not a rendering, a page or two of plan views—

OWEN AS GROPIUS: I don't have any with me—

ELLIS AS BERGER: Bring them tonight and join the party! I want to see you dance.

OWEN AS GROPIUS: Would I have to wear a costume?

BREC AS MIES VAN DER ROHE: It's Carnival. Bring only your sins.

(A flourish of dance music and lighting change puts OWEN AS GROPIUS *and* ELLIS AS BERGER *in the dark and* BREC AS MIES VAN DER ROHE *in the Carnival. He's joined by* DUCK AS KANDINSKY, *who looks annoyed and glum. Dance music continues under.)*

DUCK AS KANDINSKY: Buy a raffle ticket?

BREC AS MIES VAN DER ROHE: Wassily, some enthusiasm! How do you expect to sell without a smile?

DUCK AS KANDINSKY: Am Russian. Smile is mental defective. Or American.

BREC AS MIES VAN DER ROHE: Try again.

DUCK AS KANDINSKY: (*Fake grin*) Oh, please, sir! Buy my raffle ticket?

BREC AS MIES VAN DER ROHE: What's on raffle?

DUCK AS KANDINSKY: (*Glum again*) Artwork. By great German and Russian artists.

BREC AS MIES VAN DER ROHE: Including the brilliant Wassily Kandinsky?

DUCK AS KANDINSKY: (*Brightening*) Yes, he generously donate painting.

BREC AS MIES VAN DER ROHE: Then I will take four tickets.

DUCK AS KANDINSKY: (*Glum*) Twelve marks.

BREC AS MIES VAN DER ROHE: (*Handing over money*) Here are fifteen.

DUCK AS KANDINSKY: Is tip?

(ELLIS *appears as* FRITZ ERTL, *who has tense, high shoulders, sports a swastika armband and carries a red book with a white spine.*)

ELLIS AS ERTL: (*Peter Lorre voice*) Good evening!

DUCK AS KANDINSKY: (*Leaving*) Excuse, please.

(*Returning to the "off stage" seating,* DUCK *removes the cardigan and puts on headphones or earbuds.*)

BREC AS MIES VAN DER ROHE: Ah—it's on the tip of my tongue—you were a student—

ELLIS AS ERTL: Fritz Ertl. You signed my diploma.

BREC AS MIES VAN DER ROHE: Now I remember: Fritzi!	ELLIS AS ERTL: Now I'm a highly successful architect.

BREC AS MIES VAN DER ROHE: How are you, Fritzi?

ELLIS AS ERTL: I'm no longer your student. Please address me as Herr Ertl.

BREC AS MIES VAN DER ROHE: Of course, Fritzi. Are you here tonight to beat us up?

ELLIS AS ERTL: Rough tactics are no longer necessary now that Adolf Hitler is Chancellor.

BREC AS MIES VAN DER ROHE: Then you are evaluating us?

ELLIS AS ERTL: Perhaps I'm here to offer you a commission.

BREC AS MIES VAN DER ROHE: You have the authority?

ELLIS AS ERTL: Not yet, but imagine: the power of the Third Reich given new beauty by Bauhaus design.

BREC AS MIES VAN DER ROHE: Doesn't your party think we're all Bolsheviks?

ELLIS AS ERTL: I know the Bauhaus from inside.

BREC AS MIES VAN DER ROHE: That seems too subtle to be a Nazi threat.

ELLIS AS ERTL: It's a compliment. You yourself forced Gunta Stolzl to resign when she married a Jew. We're all on the same side now! Hitler understands art—

(BREC AS MIES VAN DER ROHE *snorts.*)

ELLIS AS ERTL: (*Showing armband*) Take the swastika, for example, which, as you know, the Fuhrer designed himself. Such bold, clean lines, energy that seems to rotate without moving because he angled it clockwise and balanced it like a diamond. Strong color contrasts, red, black, white, with perfect proportions between the circle and ground.

BREC AS MIES VAN DER ROHE: You need more than a logo to save Germany.

ELLIS AS ERTL: Exactly! Hitler also understands better than anyone how design and especially architecture can influence and even redirect human behavior. The school's never been fully supported, financially stable. Think of me as a conduit.

BREC AS MIES VAN DER ROHE: To what, exactly?

ELLIS AS ERTL: Affordable housing for workers. Isn't that a dream of yours?

BREC AS MIES VAN DER ROHE: That's Gropius' dream. I prefer high end clients.

ELLIS AS ERTL: Bauhaus palaces, then. The Fuhrer wants a Museum of German Art. What would be more Bauhaus than that?

BREC AS MIES VAN DER ROHE: What kind of art would he put in there?

ELLIS AS ERTL: Pure German art! Caspar David Friedrich, Philip Otto Runge—

BREC AS MIES VAN DER ROHE: Any living artists?

ELLIS AS ERTL: Adolf Ziegler.

BREC AS MIES VAN DER ROHE: Who?

ELLIS AS ERTL: He paints striking Aryan nudes.

BREC AS MIES VAN DER ROHE: Waxworks that communicate nothing.

ELLIS AS ERTL: Very well, Herr Director. I was hoping you'd see things differently, that I might be able to save your precious Bauhaus, but alas.

BREC AS MIES VAN DER ROHE: You could save us by buying a raffle ticket. All your old Masters contributed work. Perhaps a chance on a Kandinsky?

ELLIS AS ERTL: You're the one taking a chance. The Dessau Town Council has already contacted us about Bauhaus documentation of your relationship with that Socialist Mayor—what was his name?

BREC AS MIES VAN DER ROHE: Us, who is us?

(ELLIS AS ERTL *smiles and taps his armband.*)

BREC AS MIES VAN DER ROHE: Isn't it enough you've driven poor Hesse from office?

ELLIS AS ERTL: That's it. Mayor Hesse. Good evening.

(ELLIS AS ERTL *disappears and* OWEN AS GROPIUS *sidles up to* BREC AS MIES VAN DER ROHE.)

OWEN AS GROPIUS: Was that—?

BREC AS MIES VAN DER ROHE: Fritzi. All grown up in his Nazi pants.

OWEN AS GROPIUS: Is he spying on you?

BREC AS MIES VAN DER ROHE: A swastika armband isn't very clandestine. Of course, now they can do whatever they want in broad daylight. He tried to tempt me with a commission. Perhaps you'd like to design cost-effective worker barracks for the little corporal?

OWEN AS GROPIUS: Be cautious, my friend. Were you rude to his face?

BREC AS MIES VAN DER ROHE: He and his cohorts forced me to commit the most shameful act of my life.

OWEN AS GROPIUS: Gunta is fine. I believe she and Arieh are safe in Switzerland. Now, may I purchase a raffle ticket?

BREC AS MIES VAN DER ROHE: You're very kind, Walter. Otti Berger will eagerly sell you a ticket. In a moment I must make a pompous speech, but first, we dance.

(*Dance music really kicks in.* BREC AS MIES VAN DER ROHE *and* OWEN AS GROPIUS *do the crazy Bauhaus dance, soon joined by* ELLIS AS BERGER, DUCK AS KANDINSKY *and* KAI AS HILBERSEIMER. HILBERSEIMER *wears a pork-pie hat and chews gum.* ELLIS AS BERGER *and* KAI AS HILBERSEIMER *dance together, clearly a couple. After a while, the dance music reaches a climax and stops. A lighting change isolates*

BREC AS MIES VAN DER ROHE *in light and puts everyone else in the dark.)*

BREC AS MIES VAN DER ROHE: *(Carries rolled plans)* Ladies and gentlemen, artists and designers, patrons and friends. On the eve of Lent, a period of great solemnity and austerity, we celebrate the rebirth of the Bauhaus here in Berlin, free of government restrictions…and government support. But we have your support, the admission to the celebration and the raffle tickets you've purchased. *(Gets a glass of champagne)* I understand there are more than seven hundred of us present, so you've made the evening a great success. You have saved our school! A toast to the Berlin Bauhaus! *(Raises glass)* Now if only we can get someone to take Kandinsky's painting!

(More celebratory dance music. Lights out on BREC AS MIES VAN DER ROHE *and up on a* GESTAPO OFFICER *played by* KAI *standing guard, with a clipboard. Projected title: April 1933. Music ends abruptly as* BREC AS MIES VAN DER ROHE *appears wearing a coat and carrying rolled plans.)*

BREC AS MIES VAN DER ROHE: What is this?

KAI AS GESTAPO OFFICER: This facility is closed.

BREC AS MIES VAN DER ROHE: It's my facility. I'm the Director of this school.

KAI AS GESTAPO OFFICER: *(Consulting clipboard)* Then we have questions for you.

*(*OWEN AS RUDOLPH DIELS *brushes past them, roughly escorting* DUCK AS STUDENT. DIELS *has dueling scars on his face, wears a swastika armband and a long tie.)*

BREC AS MIES VAN DER ROHE: And what is this?

DUCK AS STUDENT: Herr Director, tell them I'm German!

Brec as Mies van der Rohe: Bahelfer! What's going on?

Owen as Diels: Not to worry, Herr Director. We are only verifying identity for students without proper papers. Protective custody.

Brec as Mies van der Rohe: Bahelfer's been a student for years and a German citizen! I can vouch for it!

Owen as Diels: Come see us at Gestapo headquarters if you have proof.

(Owen as Diels *drags* Duck as Student *away.*)

Duck as Student: Help me, Mies!

Brec as Mies van der Rohe: This is an obscenity!

(*As they disappear,* Brec as Mies van der Rohe *starts to follow.*)

Kai as Gestapo Officer: One moment, please. We're seeking evidence of financial improprieties involving Fritz Hesse, former Mayor of Dessau.

Brec as Mies van der Rohe: Yes, of course, take whatever you need. We have nothing to hide! You'll find no improprieties. Only release my student and reopen my school!

Kai as Gestapo Officer: I'm afraid not, sir. The school will remain closed until our investigation is concluded.

(*Lighting change:* Brec as Mies van der Rohe *on the telephone.*)

Brec as Mies van der Rohe: May I speak to the Reichsminister of Culture please?

(*With a slight change of costume,* Kai *becomes* Alfred Rosenberg, *a pompous Estonian bureaucrat.*)

Brec as Mies van der Rohe: Yes, Alfred Rosenberg. Tell him it's Ludwig Mies van der Rohe. He'll take my call.

KAI AS ROSENBERG: *(On phone, slight accent)* With all due respect, I'm very busy right now as you can imagine.

BREC AS MIES VAN DER ROHE: I understand, but need to speak to you immediately. Tell me when and I will be there.

KAI AS ROSENBERG: Could you come at eleven o'clock tonight?

(Lights out on KAI AS ROSENBERG *and up on* ELLIS AS BERGER *and* DUCK AS KANDINSKY. ELLIS AS BERGER *is wearing a yellow star.)*

ELLIS AS BERGER: Eleven at night?!

DUCK AS KANDINSKY: You will go into Ministry of Culture and never come out! Do not be stupid with your life.

BREC AS MIES VAN DER ROHE: If I don't go, I have nothing. If they kill me, I have nothing. I am not afraid.

ELLIS AS BERGER: Neither am I!

BREC AS MIES VAN DER ROHE: Apparently not, wearing that star just after Jewish stores were boycotted. Be more cautious, Otti!

ELLIS AS BERGER: An editorial in the Jewish Review challenged us to wear the yellow badge with pride.

DUCK AS KANDINSKY: You are Zionist?

BREC AS MIES VAN DER ROHE: That's medieval!

ELLIS AS BERGER: As an enemy of the people, I might have to be.

DUCK AS KANDINSKY: Do not joke!

BREC AS MIES VAN DER ROHE: Otti!

BREC AS MIES VAN DER ROHE: And you warn me about meeting a Nazi at night!

ELLIS AS BERGER: We'll wait across the street, there's a cafe.

DUCK AS KANDINSKY: We watch door from cafe window for you to come out, dead or alive!

(Lighting change: BREC AS MIES VAN DER ROHE *disappears and* DUCK AS KANDINSKY *and* ELLIS AS BERGER *sit down at a cafe table with cups of coffee. Alone together, they appear uncomfortable in each other's presence. Off stage,* KAI *transforms into* ROSENBERG, *but pauses to glance at a phone, scrolling through emails.)*

DUCK AS KANDINSKY: Cup is terrible.

ELLIS AS BERGER: Ask for a fresh pot.

DUCK AS KANDINSKY: No, cup design. Gewgaws and furbelows!

ELLIS AS BERGER: Your German has improved, Herr Kandinsky.

DUCK AS KANDINSKY: Is ugly, yes?

ELLIS AS BERGER: Repulsive.

(They drink. KAI *stops on an email. It's bad news.* KAI *is stunned and sits down.)*

DUCK AS KANDINSKY: I am wanting ask you question.

ELLIS AS BERGER: Yes, I'm dating Hilberseimer. Everyone wants to know!

DUCK AS KANDINSKY: That is not question. Everybody already know.

ELLIS AS BERGER: What question then?

DUCK AS KANDINSKY: The Jewish question.

(Off stage, BREC *finds the disconsolate* KAI, *who shows* BREC *the phone.* BREC *reacts with shock.* BREC *and* KAI *hold each other, fearful.)*

ELLIS AS BERGER: I'm Jewish. That's the answer.

DUCK AS KANDINSKY: No, no, I am awkward but try to understand. Did you meet Arnold Schönberg when he visit Bauhaus?

ELLIS AS BERGER: He came to Weimar, didn't he? I didn't start until Dessau.

DUCK AS KANDINSKY: My best friend since Blue Rider.

ELLIS AS BERGER: Schönberg never came to Dessau.

DUCK AS KANDINSKY: No. My fault, I think.

ELLIS AS BERGER: Ah, the Christian question.

DUCK AS KANDINSKY: There is no Christian question!

ELLIS AS BERGER: Did you offend him?

(*Off stage,* OWEN *sees* BREC *and* KAI, *who show* OWEN *the phone.* OWEN *reacts with great shock.*)

OWEN: Oh, my God!

DUCK AS KANDINSKY: (*Trying to ignore* OWEN) I state only truth and logic, very honest, but he stop writing.

ELLIS AS BERGER: Maybe your truth is not his.

DUCK AS KANDINSKY: What is truth?

(*Stunned and somewhat mechanically,* BREC *and* OWEN *help* KAI *finish transforming into* ROSENBERG.)

ELLIS AS BERGER: That is both a Christian and a Jewish question.

(*They laugh.*)

DUCK AS KANDINSKY: I worry for him. And you! With clown Chancellor, anything could happen.

ELLIS AS BERGER: I can always go back to Yugoslavia where the Nazis can't get me. What will you do?

DUCK AS KANDINSKY: I am not Jew!

ELLIS AS BERGER: Worse, you're Russian! A most dangerous foreigner.

DUCK AS KANDINSKY: I am not Communist!

ELLIS AS BERGER: Maybe you should go around like a beggar with a plaque that declares you're neither Jew nor Communist.

(DUCK AS KANDINSKY *gasps.*)

ELLIS AS BERGER: What?

DUCK AS KANDINSKY: Is what Schönberg said!

(Lighting change: BREC AS MIES VAN DER ROHE *alone with* KAI AS ROSENBERG, *who sits at a sad little desk with a cane leaning against it.* ROSENBERG *is elderly, with a bowler hat and a swastika armband.* BREC AS MIES VAN DER ROHE *holds rolled-up plans.)*

KAI AS ROSENBERG: There really is no point in your coming. All the students have already been released.

BREC AS MIES VAN DER ROHE: But the Bauhaus is locked up! As Minister of Culture, surely you understand what a blow that is to Germany right now, an international black eye!

KAI AS ROSENBERG: Of course I understand. I trained as an architect in Riga before I became a writer.

BREC AS MIES VAN DER ROHE: Then you understand that the Bauhaus is aesthetic, not political.

KAI AS ROSENBERG: With all due respect, I think it is you who do not understand.

BREC AS MIES VAN DER ROHE: Now that the National Socialists run the government, your cultural policy must support the best German institutions. It's a critical time for the aesthetic questions posed by technical and industrial development.

KAI AS ROSENBERG: Aren't these questions addressed by the Institutes of Technology?

BREC AS MIES VAN DER ROHE: No, the disciplines at the Institutes don't communicate with each other. At the Bauhaus all the arts and design work together, a *gesamtkunstwerk*!

KAI AS ROSENBERG: Ah, such jargon!

BREC AS MIES VAN DER ROHE: Moreover, each teacher at the Institutes has a hundred and fifty students. At the Bauhaus, I have three terms of thirty students each receiving personalized instruction.

KAI AS ROSENBERG: We don't want to stifle private initiative. If you're doing so well, why do you need government backing?

BREC AS MIES VAN DER ROHE: I don't need backing. I need lack of interference, I need peace.

KAI AS ROSENBERG: Is your work obstructed?

BREC AS MIES VAN DER ROHE: By a locked door! Yes!

KAI AS ROSENBERG: I am not ignorant, Herr Director. I know what the Bauhaus stands for and who works there. It represents forces fighting our forces.

BREC AS MIES VAN DER ROHE: We're not fighting— we're designing!

KAI AS ROSENBERG: But design is everything, don't you agree?

BREC AS MIES VAN DER ROHE: Yes, of course, everything human is designed—

KAI AS ROSENBERG: When you moved to Berlin, why didn't you simply change the name? That would have erased all the negative connotations at once.

BREC AS MIES VAN DER ROHE: We like our connotations! And the Bauhaus is a wonderful name, perfect for what we do.

KAI AS ROSENBERG: With all due respect, we don't like what you do.

BREC AS MIES VAN DER ROHE: You sit here in an important position, but look at your desk, a shabby little writing table. Do you enjoy this table? I would throw it out the window. That's what we do at the Bauhaus. We create beautiful, practical objects we don't have to throw out the window.

KAI AS ROSENBERG: Well. *(Struggles to his feet, using cane)* I will see what I can do.

(Lighting change: BREC AS MIES VAN DER ROHE *approaches* DUCK AS KANDINSKY *and* ELLIS AS BERGER *in the cafe.)*

DUCK AS KANDINSKY: What did he say?

ELLIS AS BERGER: May we reopen?

BREC AS MIES VAN DER ROHE: Inconclusive.

DUCK AS KANDINSKY: He not kill you at least.

ELLIS AS BERGER: You had to try. Thank you, Herr Director.

BREC AS MIES VAN DER ROHE: What is the moral responsibility of design?

*(*DUCK AS KANDINSKY *and* ELLIS AS BERGER *look at each other, confused.)*

DUCK AS KANDINSKY: To be good, nothing more. Same as art.

BREC AS MIES VAN DER ROHE: What is good?

*(*DUCK AS KANDINSKY *and* ELLIS AS BERGER *burst out laughing.)*

BREC AS MIES VAN DER ROHE: Why's that funny? It's a legitimate question.

DUCK AS KANDINSKY:	ELLIS AS BERGER:
It's a Christian question!	It's a Jewish question!

(Lighting change and title: Gestapo Headquarters, July 1933. Brec as Mies van der Rohe *is in the office of Gestapo chief* Rudolph Diels, *played by* Owen. *Throughout,* Diels *casually does clever pencil tricks.)*

Brec as Mies van der Rohe: Clever thing you've done with your waiting room furniture.

Owen as Diels: What is that?

Brec as Mies van der Rohe: The bench is only four inches wide, deliberately uncomfortable, so people give up waiting for you and go home.

Owen as Diels: Yet here you are.

Brec as Mies van der Rohe: I've been coming every day for three months. Cultural Minister Rosenberg said he'd help, but nothing's changed. I humbly request you unseal my school, which has been closed since April.

Owen as Diels: Yes, I am familiar with the Bauhaus, very interested.

Brec as Mies van der Rohe: Then you know the school is private property. We haven't stolen anything, we aren't making revolution. What's the reason we've been closed?

Owen as Diels: Kandinsky.

Brec as Mies van der Rohe: Kandinsky? What about Kandinsky?

Owen as Diels: I understand the Bauhaus, we all do, I think. You have to admire it, such international prominence so quickly. But we don't understand Kandinsky.

Brec as Mies van der Rohe: There's nothing political about Kandinsky. He's not a Communist—the Bolsheviks starved his child, he hates them.

Owen as Diels: Not his politics, his art.

BREC AS MIES VAN DER ROHE: He invented abstraction!

OWEN AS DIELS: Precisely. Which no one understands. Some claim to, but that's just pretension. The emperor's new clothes. The point of art is to communicate, that we understand very well, but if no one understands abstraction, what good is it?

BREC AS MIES VAN DER ROHE: Kandinsky himself explained abstract theory perfectly in his book, *Concerning the Spiritual in Art*.

OWEN AS DIELS: We've burnt that book. His theories are dangerous. He's too independent.

BREC AS MIES VAN DER ROHE: I personally vouch for Kandinsky. He's not a threat to you.

OWEN AS DIELS: Fine. But if anything happens, we'll hold you responsible. You're the one who will be picked up. Am I making myself clear?

BREC AS MIES VAN DER ROHE: Absolutely. So you'll allow us to reopen.

OWEN AS DIELS: Once our investigation concludes, if our findings show no improprieties—

BREC AS MIES VAN DER ROHE: We've opened all our records.

OWEN AS DIELS: *We've* opened your records. The investigation is less about the Bauhaus than the former Mayor of Dessau.

BREC AS MIES VAN DER ROHE: Fritz Hesse, yes, a wonderful friend to us.

OWEN AS DIELS: Nowadays one must choose friends wisely. Hesse was arrested last week.

BREC AS MIES VAN DER ROHE: What for?

OWEN AS DIELS: Socialism. And we've found evidence of corruption, including unusual expenses he authorized for the Bauhaus.

BREC AS MIES VAN DER ROHE: What expenses?

OWEN AS DIELS: *(Showing papers)* Repairing a leaky roof at the Bauhaus facility in Dessau.

BREC AS MIES VAN DER ROHE: That was legitimate. When Gropius designed the building, he experimented with materials. We've always had terrible leaks.

OWEN AS DIELS: *(Nods, reading)* Construction is not to blame, but design and choice of materials. The flat cement slab roof is not flexible and fails to sufficiently expand and contract with changes in temperature. Crews work on the roof for weeks and there is slight improvement, but at the first hard rain the buckets under leaks fill to the brim overnight.

BREC AS MIES VAN DER ROHE: Experiments do not always work, but they point to progress.

OWEN AS DIELS: For a thousand years German roofs have been designed with peaks so rain and snow slide off. Peasants know this. Your flat Bauhaus roofs are designed for a dry, Oriental climate, not here.

BREC AS MIES VAN DER ROHE: Oriental?

OWEN AS DIELS: Palestinian.

BREC AS MIES VAN DER ROHE: Are you saying our roofs are Jewish?

OWEN AS DIELS: You have Jewish instructors.

BREC AS MIES VAN DER ROHE: None, actually, at present.

OWEN AS DIELS: But Jewish students.

BREC AS MIES VAN DER ROHE: That does not mean our roofs are circumcised.

OWEN AS DIELS: Just leaky.

BREC AS MIES VAN DER ROHE: We learned from that roof. I employ flat roofs in my own designs, and they don't leak. It was just a matter of finding the right materials, as your report indicates.

OWEN AS DIELS: We needn't debate, Herr Director. I'm on your side and will do everything I can to reopen the Bauhaus. Next week I am speaking with Hermann Göring about conditions.

BREC AS MIES VAN DER ROHE: Next week! That's wonderful. What conditions?

OWEN AS DIELS: He will tell me, I'm sure. I admire not only the Bauhaus but your patience with my waiting room bench.

BREC AS MIES VAN DER ROHE: We'd be happy to redesign that for you.

OWEN AS DIELS: It suits its purpose. One other thing.

BREC AS MIES VAN DER ROHE: Yes?

OWEN AS DIELS: As you may have heard, the Fuhrer plans significant investment in infrastructure, including camps for workers and a new museum, a house for German art. Your name was floated.

BREC AS MIES VAN DER ROHE: That's an enormous compliment. Would I have to peak the roof?

OWEN AS DIELS: I'm utterly serious. Hitler wants the museum open by the Olympics to show the world Germany is resurrecting from the disaster of the war. Gropius is another name mentioned.

BREC AS MIES VAN DER ROHE: Either way, Bauhaus.

OWEN AS DIELS: Precisely. It's time for the Bauhaus to choose new friends.

(Lights out on them and up on ELLIS AS HITLER *making a speech.)*

ELLIS AS HITLER: The loss of the war in 1918 revealed the slime and corruption of German society, a body rotten in both politics and culture. But what does it mean to be German? To be German is simply to be clear, to be logical and true.

(Lights up on BREC AS MIES VAN DER ROHE *as* DUCK AS STUDENT *brings him a letter in a green envelope.* BREC AS MIES VAN DER ROHE *puts the rolled plans under his arm, opens the letter and reads it to himself while* DUCK AS STUDENT *watches.)*

ELLIS AS HITLER: True German art reflects the German people, not fashionable foreign deceptions like Cubism, Dadaism, Futurism, Impressionism. The new Germany will not tolerate such weak and meaningless words. We must not go backward, worshipping "primitive" art lauded by pre-history art stutterers, images of cripples and cretins, repulsive women, and children cursed by God. These so-called artists either suffer from visual defects—and defects must be purged from a healthy German state—or they deliberately deceive and confuse the public, which constitutes cultural crime. Either way, such criminals and defectives will no longer exist in the new German Reich!

(Lights out on ELLIS AS HITLER*)*

BREC AS MIES VAN DER ROHE: Order champagne.

DUCK AS STUDENT: Good news?

BREC AS MIES VAN DER ROHE: From the Gestapo, believe it or not.

DUCK AS STUDENT: We can reopen the school?

BREC AS MIES VAN DER ROHE: Invite the faculty immediately, everyone who's available: Kandinsky,

Hilberseimer, Albers, Peterhans, Otti Berger if you can track her down.

(DUCK AS STUDENT *disappears, and faculty begin to gather:* KAI AS HILBERSEIMER *and* ELLIS AS BERGER *are the first to arrive with champagne glasses, including an extra one for* BREC AS MIES VAN DER ROHE.)

ELLIS AS BERGER: Is it true?

KAI AS HILBERSEIMER: I won't believe it till I see it.

BREC AS MIES VAN DER ROHE: *(Flourishing the green envelope)* Here's the letter. Official word.

KAI AS HILBERSEIMER: *(Reaching for letter)* May I?

BREC AS MIES VAN DER ROHE: *(Pocketing the letter)* Champagne first!

(BREC AS MIES VAN DER ROHE *opens champagne and fills their glasses.)*

ELLIS AS BERGER: No fair for you to keep us in suspense!

KAI AS HILBERSEIMER: Have we, in fact, received permission?

BREC AS MIES VAN DER ROHE: We're celebrating! That much I can tell you.

ELLIS AS BERGER: *(To* KAI AS HILBERSEIMER*)* Ludwig, darling, be patient!

(DUCK AS KANDINSKY *arrives with a champagne glass.)*

DUCK AS KANDINSKY: What is meaning of champagne?

ELLIS AS BERGER: Mies won't say!

DUCK AS KANDINSKY: Reopen Bauhaus or not?

BREC AS MIES VAN DER ROHE: Enjoy your champagne. I'm not saying anything until we're all assembled.

KAI AS HILBERSEIMER: On short notice, that will be hard.

BREC AS MIES VAN DER ROHE: Trust me! We have reason to celebrate!

(They all drink their champagne quietly while OWEN AS DIELS *appears isolated in light holding another version of the letter in the green envelope.)*

OWEN AS DIELS: *(Reading letter)* Dear Director Mies van der Rohe: It is with great pleasure that I inform you of our decision regarding the Bauhaus school.

DUCK AS KANDINSKY: You know, I am almost out of money.

BREC AS MIES VAN DER ROHE: You're always almost out of money!

(They laugh.)

OWEN AS DIELS: The Reich Ministry of Culture has authorized the Gestapo to unseal the Bauhaus building in Berlin so the school may begin classes again as soon as is practical.

ELLIS AS BERGER: If there's enough money, maybe I can come back to teach!

OWEN AS DIELS: We will undertake the unsealing action as soon as the following conditions have been met and verified.

KAI AS HILBERSEIMER: I'm astonished the Nazis would have this change of heart.

ELLIS AS BERGER: Heart? Where did you get that idea?

OWEN AS DIELS: The employment of abstract Bolshevik artist Wassily Kandinsky must be terminated.

DUCK AS KANDINSKY: Berlin getting too expensive with no Reichsmarks!

OWEN AS DIELS: Similarly, the employment of Democratic Socialist architect Ludwig Hilberseimer will be terminated.

KAI AS HILBERSEIMER: Mies, will we see more cooperation between your architecture office and the Bauhaus now that we're all in Berlin?

BREC AS MIES VAN DER ROHE: Possibly.

OWEN AS DIELS: Termination of these two employees must take place at once, with appropriate documentation.

BREC AS MIES VAN DER ROHE: I was hoping more faculty could join us, but I believe we must proceed in any case.

OWEN AS DIELS: The third condition is in accordance with proposed future regulations of the German state.

BREC AS MIES VAN DER ROHE: *(Showing green envelope)* Here is a letter from the Gestapo authorizing us to reopen the Bauhaus.

(Applause)

KAI AS HILBERSEIMER: ELLIS AS BERGER:
Fantastic!   How wonderful!

DUCK AS KANDINSKY: I do not believe it!

OWEN AS DIELS: We have documented a total of sixteen Jews among the current student body of the Bauhaus.

BREC AS MIES VAN DER ROHE: I visited the Gestapo office every other day for three months trying to get this letter. I was most anxious about it and wanted official permission for us to proceed.

OWEN AS DIELS: All Jewish students of the Bauhaus must be expelled immediately.

BREC AS MIES VAN DER ROHE: We now have that permission, subject to certain conditions.

KAI AS HILBERSEIMER: What conditions?

ELLIS AS BERGER: Surely they'll be easy to fulfill.	DUCK AS KANDINSKY: Always there are conditions.

BREC AS MIES VAN DER ROHE: I would like to make a proposition, and I hope you'll agree with me.

OWEN AS DIELS: Congratulations on this determination. The German government looks forward to continued success for the Bauhaus and future collaboration for the glory of the Third Reich.

BREC AS MIES VAN DER ROHE: I would like to write them a letter in response, saying "Thank you very much for permission to open the school again—"

OWEN AS DIELS: Yours sincerely, Rudolf Diels, Chief, Gestapo.

BREC AS MIES VAN DER ROHE: "But the faculty has decided to close it."

(ELLIS AS BERGER *gasps. Silence among the faculty for a moment. Light remains on* OWEN AS DIELS, *as if he awaits an answer.*)

DUCK AS KANDINSKY: I do not understand.

KAI AS HILBERSEIMER: Is this because of the conditions?	ELLIS AS BERGER: Oh, I think I understand.

BREC AS MIES VAN DER ROHE: Shall we have a vote to make it official?

KAI AS HILBERSEIMER: Wait, what?

ELLIS AS BERGER: Yes! All those in favor of closing the Bauhaus—

DUCK AS KANDINSKY: Immediately?	KAI AS HILBERSEIMER: What are the conditions?

BREC AS MIES VAN DER ROHE: And permanently.

ELLIS AS BERGER: Please raise your hand.

(BREC AS MIES VAN DER ROHE *and* ELLIS AS BERGER *immediately raise their hands.* KAI AS HILBERSEIMER *takes a moment longer, and hugs* ELLIS AS BERGER *while he raises his hand. Lights out on* OWEN AS DIELS.*)*

DUCK AS KANDINSKY: *(Raising hand)* There is nothing more to it, then?

(BREC AS MIES VAN DER ROHE *sets down the rolled plans.*)

BREC AS MIES VAN DER ROHE: Now, a toast. To the Bauhaus!

(They raise their glasses.)

KAI AS HILBERSEIMER: Prost!

ELLIS AS BERGER & DUCK AS KANDINSKY: To the Bauhaus!

ELLIS AS BERGER: And to our Director—

BREC AS MIES VAN DER ROHE: Former Director!

ELLIS AS BERGER: Ludwig Mies van der Rohe! For the courage to seek a yes, and the courage to say no.

DUCK AS KANDINSKY: To our Director!

ELLIS AS BERGER: Herr Director!

KAI AS HILBERSEIMER: To Mies!

(They all raise their glasses and freeze. Music by Arnold Schönberg plays. Lights out on them, but a spot remains on the abandoned plans. A montage of photographic images whips by: Bauhaus historic photographs [faculty, students, buildings], Bauhaus products in all media, ending with the gate of Buchenwald's beautiful Bauhaus letters proclaiming "Jedem das seine" [to each his own]. As the montage plays over them, the STUDENTS *transform the set in view of the audience. The rolled plans disappears in darkness.)*

OWEN: Of course, the end of the Bauhaus in 1933—

ELLIS: —Wasn't the end!

KAI: *(Bitterly)* It is for me.

BREC: We've shown you the gods of the Bauhaus—

ELLIS: But also their feet of clay.

DUCK: Now we show Bauhaus diaspora—immigrants!

KAI: Right here in Los Angeles.

(Lights out on the transformed environment, and a title in the darkness: Los Angeles, Friday, July 13, 1951. Thunder. After a moment lights come up on a mid-century modern showroom featuring many shelves of textile samples, drapes covering floor-to-ceiling windows, two "Wassily" club chairs and one Barcelona chair [the setting need not be realistic except for the chairs and some textiles]. MARIA KIPP, 51, played by BREC, and ZENOBIO REMEDIOS, 47, played by DUCK, stand holding buckets. KIPP wears a professional skirt and blouse and has excellent posture. REMEDIOS wears a short-sleeved knit shirt.)

DUCK AS REMEDIOS: *Ay, Dios mio.*

BREC AS KIPP: *(German accent)* It's July!

DUCK AS REMEDIOS: It doesn't rain in Los Angeles in July!

(As REMEDIOS walks, it's apparent he has a limp. BREC AS KIPP lays out some fabric samples.)

BREC AS KIPP: Only in our studio. Hide the buckets. Maybe it's just heat lightning.

DUCK AS REMEDIOS: *(Hiding the buckets)* That's not very subtle.

BREC AS KIPP: I'm just choosing. We'll keep the samples hidden unless they ask. Start with champagne…

(She hides the samples. Offstage, OWEN helps ELLIS change costumes.)

DUCK AS REMEDIOS: How many glasses?

BREC AS KIPP: Three of them and two of us.

DUCK AS REMEDIOS: Three? The architect, the composer and who else? (*Fetches champagne glasses.*)

BREC AS KIPP: I can't imagine she'll actually come, but the three of them in the same room—!

DUCK AS REMEDIOS: The composer won't buy anything.

BREC AS KIPP: Probably not, but Schönberg is how I got Gropius to come, and he's the one with the prefabricated housing company in Burbank—

DUCK AS REMEDIOS: The big prize!

BREC AS KIPP: Don't you make fun of me, Zeno! If General Panel Corporation contracts for our upholstery and drapes in their mass produced homes, we'll be set for five years, maybe longer.

(*Finishing the costume change,* OWEN *steps back to admire* ELLIS' *transformation. After a moment,* OWEN *almost shyly leans in and gives* ELLIS *a quick kiss.*)

DUCK AS REMEDIOS: And if he isn't interested?

BREC AS KIPP: She's also influential. She has a salon.

(*Astonished by the kiss,* ELLIS *stares at* OWEN *in confusion. Then suddenly they start making out.* KAI *sees them but sneaks away before they notice.*)

DUCK AS REMEDIOS: Do they know she's invited?

BREC AS KIPP: I met them all once, thirty years ago. Only Gropius is likely to remember me.

(OWEN *and* ELLIS *stop making out and finish getting into costume, suddenly shy of each other.*)

DUCK AS REMEDIOS: And now you own the studio. So they don't know she's going to be here.

BREC AS KIPP: Be sure to mention Schindler and Neutra are clients. If I do, they'll think I'm puffing myself up.

DUCK AS REMEDIOS: Is Gropius bigger than Schindler?

BREC AS KIPP: He's international! Teaches at Harvard! Schindler and Neutra are local only.

DUCK AS REMEDIOS: I've never seen you nervous before.

BREC AS KIPP: This may very well be the most important client meeting of my life! (*Shows sample*) Everything about this I learned in a few weeks at the Bauhaus.

DUCK AS REMEDIOS: Nervous and sentimental.

BREC AS KIPP: I am missing Germany a little bit, maybe.

DUCK AS REMEDIOS: I'm not.

(*Door chimes.* BREC AS KIPP *rushes to the door and opens it.* OWEN AS GROPIUS, 68, and KAI AS SCHÖNBERG, 76, greet BREC AS KIPP *formally, shaking hands.* OWEN AS GROPIUS *wears a hat.* KAI AS SCHÖNBERG *wears a suitcoat and his eyes tend to bug out.*)

OWEN AS GROPIUS: *Guten tag, Frau Kipp!*

KAI AS SCHÖNBERG: (*Smoking a cigarette*) *Es ist mir eine Ehre, Ihre Bekanntschaft zu machen!* [Honored to make your acquaintance!]

(BREC AS KIPP *brings them into the room.*)

BREC AS KIPP: *Wilkommen!* (*Gestures toward* DUCK AS REMEDIOS *and the audience*) But we must speak English for the benefit of the audience!

(OWEN AS GROPIUS *puts both index fingers to temples.*)

KAI AS SCHÖNBERG:	OWEN AS GROPIUS:
(*Looking at audience*)	What audience?
Was meinst du?	
[What do you mean?]	

BREC AS KIPP: May I introduce Zenobio Remedios, manager of Maria Kipp Hand Loomed Drapery and Upholstery Fabrics.

KAI AS SCHÖNBERG: *(Shaking hands)* My pleasure, Mr Remedios. I am Arnold Schönberg.

OWEN AS GROPIUS: *(Shaking)* Walter Gropius, please excuse the German. We don't get so often to use it these days.

DUCK AS REMEDIOS: *¡Mucho gusto!*

BREC AS KIPP: *¡No te burles!* [Don't make fun!]

DUCK AS REMEDIOS: *¡No me estoy burlando!* [I'm not making fun!] Mrs Kipp has been telling me about your music and your architecture.

OWEN AS GROPIUS: She can explain your music?

KAI AS SCHÖNBERG: More easily than your architecture! *(To* BREC AS KIPP*) Wo ist die Toilette bitte?* [Where is the toilet, please?]

BREC AS KIPP: Upstairs. Zeno, would you please show Herr Schönberg the facilities?

DUCK AS REMEDIOS: Of course! This way, sir.

(As they leave:)

KAI AS SCHÖNBERG: It was a long drive from Brentwood and I am seventy-six years old!

BREC AS KIPP: Please sit down.

OWEN AS GROPIUS: *(Sees the "Wassily" chairs)* Oh.

BREC AS KIPP: Yes, Breuer's chairs. My studio is modern in every way.

OWEN AS GROPIUS: I prefer the Barcelona, actually.

*(*OWEN AS GROPIUS *sits in the Barcelona chair and* BREC AS KIPP *in one of the Wassily chairs.)*

OWEN AS GROPIUS: This building, is it new?

BREC AS KIPP: We only opened a few weeks ago.

OWEN AS GROPIUS: I like the way the street windows echo the clerestory roof.

BREC AS KIPP: You don't remember me, do you?

OWEN AS GROPIUS: *(Finger to temple)* Oh, dear. I'm afraid not. You were a Bauhaus student?

BREC AS KIPP: I thought perhaps you came today because you remembered.

OWEN AS GROPIUS: Oh. Oh! From the *Munchen Kunstgewerbeschule* where Gunta studied?

BREC AS KIPP: You remember!

OWEN AS GROPIUS: How could I forget—most unfortunate—

(Door chimes.)

OWEN AS GROPIUS: You are expecting maybe someone else?

BREC AS KIPP: Yes, a little surprise.

(BREC AS KIPP *opens the door, admitting* ELLIS AS MAHLER, *72, overdone, carrying a purse.)*

ELLIS AS MAHLER: *Gott in Himmel!* It is so humid! What have you to drink?

BREC AS KIPP: Hello, we have champagne—

ELLIS AS MAHLER: Benedictine! I adore Benedictine!

BREC AS KIPP: You must be Frau Werfel.

ELLIS AS MAHLER: Yes, I am the widow Werfel, but please call me Alma. Alma Mahler is how most people know me—

OWEN AS GROPIUS: So. Alma. You're my surprise.

ELLIS AS MAHLER: Gropius, darling, I had no idea!

OWEN AS GROPIUS: No idea at all?

ELLIS AS MAHLER: *(Lying)* None! I really do need that drink.

BREC AS KIPP: I'll open the champagne. *(She does.)*

OWEN AS GROPIUS: You should call yourself Alma Gropius, since I'm your only husband still who survives.

ELLIS AS MAHLER: Mahler was my most talented husband. Artistically.

(BREC AS KIPP *gives them champagne.*)

OWEN AS GROPIUS: (*Fingers to temples*) Alma enjoys always to shock people. Apparently you do, as well. Who else is coming, Leni Riefenstahl?

(KAI AS SCHÖNBERG *returning with* DUCK AS REMEDIOS*:*)

KAI AS SCHÖNBERG: Alma! *Mein Gott!*

ELLIS AS MAHLER: Schönberg! Darling! (*Greets him with cheek kisses*) Is this to be a salon? Frau Kipp, you mustn't try to compete with me. I give the best salons. (*Sees* DUCK AS REMEDIOS) And who is this, your Latin lover?

DUCK AS ZENOBIO: Zenobio Remedios.

(DUCK AS REMEDIOS *tries to shake* ELLIS AS MAHLER*'s hand, but she kisses him, too.*)

DUCK AS ZENOBIO: I'm the manager here.

ELLIS AS MAHLER: Where did you find him?

BREC AS KIPP: Just down the block, actually. He used to manage a spa.

OWEN AS GROPIUS: (*Re: champagne*) This hits right the spot!

ELLIS AS MAHLER: More champagne, please, so much to celebrate!

(DUCK AS REMEDIOS *fills her glass*)

ELLIS AS MAHLER: Are you Catholic?

DUCK AS ZENOBIO: At one time.

ELLIS AS MAHLER: Did you see my husband's motion picture, *Song of Bernadette*? The most Catholic of novels written by a Jew.

DUCK AS ZENOBIO: Your husband was Franz Werfel?

ELLIS AS MAHLER: He knows Franz!

DUCK AS ZENOBIO: Everyone who loves movies knows *Song of Bernadette*. Jennifer Jones won Best Actress!

ELLIS AS MAHLER: You're not married, Señor Remedios?

DUCK AS ZENOBIO:
No, almost a few years ago—

OWEN AS GROPIUS:
Alma, he's half your age!

KAI AS SCHÖNBERG:
Half a world away and thirty years later, no change!

ELLIS AS MAHLER:
Mahler was nineteen years older than me, and Werfel eleven years younger.

ELLIS AS MAHLER: Franz was a Jew, but I buried him Catholic. Of course I didn't attend, I couldn't bear it. That wasn't his only motion picture, you know. He wrote also *Juarez*, based on his play.

(DUCK AS REMEDIOS *laughs*.)

ELLIS AS MAHLER: Why are you laughing? Why is he laughing? It was nominated for an Academy Award!

DUCK AS ZENOBIO: Paul Muni played Juarez.

ELLIS AS MAHLER: So? He was very talented.

DUCK AS ZENOBIO: At make-up. The whitest Oaxacan ever!

ELLIS AS MAHLER: Well, aren't you spicy?

(KAI AS SCHÖNBERG *lights up another cigarette, basically smoking throughout*.)

ELLIS AS MAHLER: You can make it up to me yet with more champagne. *(He pours.)* So what is this place, really?

BREC AS KIPP: My weaving studio. We make hand-loomed fabrics like at the Bauhaus.

DUCK AS REMEDIOS: Schindler and Neutra are clients.

ELLIS AS MAHLER: Ah, I see. You were Gropius' student at the Bauhaus?

BREC AS KIPP & OWEN AS GROPIUS: No—

BREC AS KIPP: Itten's. Briefly.

ELLIS AS MAHLER: Itten. Well, that explains it.

BREC AS KIPP: I met you all there at a party around 1920. I don't expect you remember me, but I thought with three of us living in Los Angeles and Director Gropius in town on business—

ELLIS AS MAHLER: We'd have a *kleine Deutsche* reunion. How very nice. Schönberg and I see each other all the time, but Gropius, when was it?

OWEN AS GROPIUS: Before the war.

ELLIS AS MAHLER: And here we all are in America! The opposite of Germany! Franz had to flee, of course, after they burned his books, so I came with him to Los Angeles, the opposite of Berlin! Schönberg, you converted to Protestant, so you would have been safe.

KAI AS SCHÖNBERG: I was still a Jew in Hitler's eyes, so I converted back and emigrated.

ELLIS AS MAHLER: And when did you come? Kipp is a Jewish name, isn't it?

OWEN AS GROPIUS:	BREC AS KIPP:
Alma, why do you need to know?	No.

ELLIS AS MAHLER: How can you understand someone without knowing their religion? It's like not knowing their race, their sex, who they like to sleep with. Fundamental!

DUCK AS REMEDIOS: More champagne?

KAI AS SCHÖNBERG: OWEN AS GROPIUS:
God, yes!   Yes, please.

(DUCK AS REMEDIOS *fills their glasses.* ELLIS AS MAHLER *just holds hers out imperiously and he fills it after sneaking a glance at* BREC AS KIPP, *who nods.*)

ELLIS AS MAHLER: Not Jewish, then why did you leave Germany? You are communist?

BREC AS KIPP: Herr Gropius knows.

OWEN AS GROPIUS: I do? Oh! Yes, I believe I do. Itten turned you Mazdaznan!

BREC AS KIPP: The world headquarters of Mazdaznan is here in Los Angeles.

ELLIS AS MAHLER: BREC AS KIPP:
A very peculiar religion,   I've since given it up.
as I recall it. Those silly
robes, the bizarre diet?

BREC AS KIPP: A central belief of Mazdaznan is the superiority of the white race. Living in Hollywood disabused me of that notion.

KAI AS SCHÖNBERG: Hitler disabused us of that notion as well.

ELLIS AS MAHLER: Hitler had some very good notions, just took them a little too far.

KAI AS SCHÖNBERG: You defend Hitler when you had to flee him?

OWEN AS GROPIUS: Like Hitler, Alma also is a failed artist. They could not create, so they destroy.

ELLIS AS MAHLER: I didn't have to flee, my Jewish husband did, and I went with him out of loyalty, because that's the kind of woman I am.

(OWEN AS GROPIUS *snorts.*)

ELLIS AS MAHLER: I even told Franz the Germans would win because they were superior, which they would have, if not for the Americans.

BREC AS KIPP: Zeno fought in the Rainbow Division.

ELLIS AS MAHLER: If you fought in Europe, darling, then you know the Germans are superior.

KAI AS SCHÖNBERG: Even if he beat them?

DUCK AS REMEDIOS: I'm sure the Germans…as a people…are a fine group. Like yourselves.

ELLIS AS MAHLER: But we're not all of us German! Schönberg is Austrian, as am I also. Very different from Germans!

KAI AS SCHÖNBERG: Yes, the Germans are Protestant anti-Semites and the Austrians are Catholic anti-Semites.

ELLIS AS MAHLER: Americans are more German than anything else.

OWEN AS GROPIUS: The best of us came here, I like to think—

ELLIS AS MAHLER: Genetically, the cream—

KAI AS SCHÖNBERG: *Mein Gott,* I've emigrated from one anti-Semitic country to another. At least I'm not a *schwartzer.*

BREC AS KIPP: But we're all equal in this country, all immigrants.

ELLIS AS MAHLER: Like you, Señor Remedios!

DUCK AS REMEDIOS: I was born here in Los Angeles.

BREC AS KIPP: *(Can't help it)* Herr Director, would you like to see some textile samples?

ELLIS AS MAHLER: I may be Viennese, but I'm in the fight of my life with the Austrian government this very day!

KAI AS SCHÖNBERG: The fight of your life? What about?

ELLIS AS MAHLER: *(Pulls a photo from her purse)* This!

*(*KAI AS SCHÖNBERG *and* DUCK AS REMEDIOS *look at the image.)*

OWEN AS GROPIUS: Your work is truly Bauhaus?

BREC AS KIPP: Well, I've been very careful not to steal any designs—

*(*BREC AS KIPP *whips out the samples she has ready.)*

DUCK AS REMEDIOS:
Is that a painting?

KAI AS SCHÖNBERG:
It's a Munch, isn't it?

ELLIS AS MAHLER:
Always so perceptive, Schönberg!

KAI AS SCHÖNBERG:
How did you come by it?

ELLIS AS MAHLER:
Ask Gropius. Gropius!

BREC AS KIPP:
But the influence is inescapable, even though I was there only briefly—

OWEN AS GROPIUS:
With Gunta. She's in Switzerland, I believe.

BREC AS KIPP:
Do you keep up with many Bauhausler?

OWEN AS GROPIUS:
It's a bit of an obsession. These are very nice. Some lovely experiments.

BREC AS KIPP:
These are drapery, of course. Would you like to see some upholstery samples?

OWEN AS GROPIUS: Pardon me. Yes, Alma?

ELLIS AS MAHLER: How did I come by this?

OWEN AS GROPIUS: Oh, the Munch! You have it still?

ELLIS AS MAHLER: My stepfather sold it to the Belvedere after the Anschluss and to get it back I've taken on the entire Austrian government.

(ELLIS AS MAHLER *watches* OWEN AS GROPIUS *engrossed in the image.*)

ELLIS AS MAHLER: You remember when you gave it to me?

OWEN AS GROPIUS: *(Tearing up)* Yes.

ELLIS AS MAHLER: *(To the others)* Upon the birth of our daughter, Manon.

OWEN AS GROPIUS: Mutzi.

ELLIS AS MAHLER: Who died of complications of polio in 1935. A gentle, beautiful girl, wanted be an actress even after she was completely paralyzed. Took after her handsome father.

(ELLIS AS MAHLER *touches* OWEN AS GROPIUS *in an intimate, gentle way. He moves away.*)

OWEN AS GROPIUS: *(Overcome)* And her beautiful mother.

ELLIS AS MAHLER: *(A step toward him)* Gropius—

OWEN AS GROPIUS: *(Moving away)* Excuse me, your lavatory?

DUCK AS REMEDIOS: I'll show you.

(They leave quickly.)

ELLIS AS MAHLER: I would not say this in front of him, but— *(Knocks back an entire glass of champagne.)* Gropius never saw her alive after he left Germany in 1932 because of government travel restrictions. He and Ise paid the penalty taxes and came to the funeral, but I stayed home. I couldn't bear it.

BREC AS KIPP: What an awful story.

ELLIS AS MAHLER: Gropius shocked me by attending. I thought the Bauhaus was really his only child.

KAI AS SCHÖNBERG: That's unkind.

ELLIS AS MAHLER: I cared for our human children virtually alone while he was midwifing, nursing and wiping the ass of the Bauhaus for nine years.

KAI AS SCHÖNBERG: You were most of that time *divorced*.

ELLIS AS MAHLER: Which made it all the more painful. Three children I've lost. We have all lost so much. You, especially, Schönberg.

KAI AS SCHÖNBERG: Thanks to your beloved Fuhrer. But let us not speak of that.

ELLIS AS MAHLER: I was thinking of your friendship with Kandinsky.

(*Thunder. They all look up,* BREC AS KIPP *with special trepidation. Off stage, but in view,* DUCK *pulls a phone out of a backpack and scrolls through messages.*)

KAI AS SCHÖNBERG: You of all people should not bring that up.

ELLIS AS MAHLER: Should I not have warned you? As your friend?

KAI AS SCHÖNBERG: Frau Kipp, your designs, may I see some?

(*Sounds of rain on the roof. Seeing something on phone,* DUCK *gives an ecstatic shriek. The others are startled but try to ignore* DUCK *and go on with their scene.*)

BREC AS KIPP: (*Showing samples*) Draperies should enhance but not distract, filter the light but let it shine through. So I keep the complicated and gathered weaves near the floor.

(*Off stage,* OWEN *goes to* DUCK, *who shows the phone.* OWEN *gives* DUCK *a big hug.*)

ELLIS AS MAHLER: Maria, is your weaving business successful? I'm not aware of your work.

BREC AS KIPP: I've sold enough to build this factory.

ELLIS AS MAHLER: So quiet for a Friday.

BREC AS KIPP: I sent the workers home early with guests coming over.

ELLIS AS MAHLER: Weaving is for women very appropriate. I was a composer, you know, until Mahler made me give it up. I didn't go to his funeral either.

KAI AS SCHÖNBERG: You couldn't bear it?

BREC AS KIPP: Everyone says your life is your art.

ELLIS AS MAHLER: I've devoted myself to artists: Klimt, Zemlinsky, Mahler, Kokoschka, Gropius, Werfel—

KAI AS SCHÖNBERG: She's a collector.

ELLIS AS MAHLER: My life is not about me at all.

BREC AS KIPP: Are you satisfied with your upholstery, with your drapes? I've heard your home is very tasteful.

(BREC AS KIPP *notices a leak and tries to be discreet putting out a bucket.*)

ELLIS AS MAHLER: You'll have to visit, perhaps assess my antimacassars.

KAI AS SCHÖNBERG: Wonderful idea! Would you be willing some day to come to Brentwood and make recommendations?

(OWEN AS GROPIUS *and* DUCK AS REMEDIOS *return, each bearing two buckets. They may be smiling inappropriately.*)

OWEN AS GROPIUS: Frau Kipp, your clerestories are leaking!

(OWEN AS GROPIUS *and* DUCK AS REMEDIOS *place the buckets. Perhaps the sounds of drips)*

BREC AS KIPP: Yes, we're just discovering that!

OWEN AS GROPIUS: We had often the same problem in Dessau! Forgive me if your distress brings back fond memories!

(ELLIS AS MAHLER *holds out her glass for more champagne. With some hesitation,* DUCK AS REMEDIOS *pours.)*

BREC AS KIPP: How embarrassing!

ELLIS AS MAHLER: Think nothing of it, Maria! All of Gropius' roofs leaked, a hallmark of modernism! *Gracias, señor.*

OWEN AS GROPIUS: Not all, Alma. We discovered it's simply a matter of materials. General Panel Corporation built a flat-roofed home in Nichols Canyon last year.

DUCK AS ZENOBIO: Does it need drapes? Maria Kipp Hand-Loomed Fabrics produced the drapes for Hollyhock House.

OWEN AS GROPIUS:	BREC AS KIPP:
Really? I met Frank Lloyd	And the upholstery!
Wright in Berlin in 1910.	

BREC AS KIPP: He was a very demanding client—

ELLIS AS MAHLER: *(Drains her glass)* Such reminiscence! How we've changed, darlings, how the world has changed!

KAI AS SCHÖNBERG: Some of us haven't changed much….

BREC AS KIPP: *(Covering* SCHÖNBERG*)* How the Bauhaus has changed the world!

OWEN AS GROPIUS: That is very kind of you to say.

ELLIS AS MAHLER: Such modesty, Gropius!

ELLIS AS MAHLER:	OWEN AS GROPIUS:
Your Bauhaus legacy is all you think about.	You need a certain humbleness—

ELLIS AS MAHLER:	OWEN AS GROPIUS:
You're one of the designosaurs!	—Not going too much into the foreground—

OWEN AS GROPIUS: But I am indeed astonished at—

KAI AS SCHÖNBERG:	OWEN AS GROPIUS:
You should be!	—What the Bauhaus managed to do—

OWEN AS GROPIUS: —In a scant fourteen years. We had sometimes big fights with each other, but the world I believe is better for it.

ELLIS AS MAHLER: Of course you must tell yourself that, darling, in the wake of its failure.

BREC AS KIPP: Herr Gropius, do you really remember every student?

ELLIS AS MAHLER: *(Signals for more champagne)* Only those he slept with.

(BREC AS KIPP *signals* DUCK AS REMEDIOS *"no more champagne for her".*)

OWEN AS GROPIUS: A significantly smaller group than those you slept with.

(KAI AS SCHÖNBERG *snorts in his glass.*)

DUCK AS ZENOBIO:	BREC AS KIPP:
Would anyone like to see our looms?	It really is impressive what your students have accomplished. Of which are you most proud?

ELLIS AS MAHLER: Herbert Bayer.

OWEN AS GROPIUS: Yes, Bayer's done very well in Aspen—

ELLIS AS MAHLER: And designing that tourist brochure for Hitler's Olympics—

OWEN AS GROPIUS: I have seen that brochure on Herbert's desk with Hitler's face scratched out—

ELLIS AS MAHLER: Only after the Nazis declared Bayer's art degenerate.

(ELLIS AS MAHLER *grabs an unattended champagne bottle and pours herself more. When she sets it down,* DUCK AS REMEDIOS *confiscates it, looks up at the dripping ceiling and leaves.*)

BREC AS KIPP: Gunta Stolzl—

OWEN AS GROPIUS: Quite well she is doing in Switzerland—

BREC AS KIPP: Other weavers—Otti Berger?

OWEN AS GROPIUS: Ah.

BREC AS KIPP: Did she go home to Yugoslavia?

OWEN AS GROPIUS: To take care of her mother. *(Hesitates)*

ELLIS AS MAHLER: Then?

BREC AS KIPP: Did she not—?

(OWEN AS GROPIUS *gestures sadly, almost as if to ward off the question.*)

ELLIS AS MAHLER: Where?

OWEN AS GROPIUS: *(Quietly)* Auschwitz.

ELLIS AS MAHLER: Which was designed by a Bauhausler.

(DUCK AS REMEDIOS *returns with two more buckets and sets them under leaks.*)

BREC AS KIPP: Surely that's not true.

KAI AS SCHÖNBERG: Shame, Alma.

ELLIS AS MAHLER: Fritz Ertl. I am correct, Gropius, yes?

(ELLIS AS MAHLER *finds a second bottle of champagne and pours for herself. When* DUCK AS REMEDIOS *tries to take it away,* ELLIS AS MAHLER *quietly but obviously gropes him.* DUCK AS REMEDIOS *moves away.* ELLIS AS MAHLER *follows almost stealthily.)*

OWEN AS GROPIUS: He designed some barracks and the crematoria.

KAI AS SCHÖNBERG: *Mein Gott.*

ELLIS AS MAHLER: His gas chambers he called "bathing facilities for special actions."

OWEN AS GROPIUS: You bestir yourself to learn such a thing?

ELLIS AS MAHLER: I find myself fascinated with the morality of artists, of designers. Speer's architecture served the Third Reich—

OWEN AS GROPIUS: And was hideous.

ELLIS AS MAHLER: Leni Riefenstahl, also a tool of fascism—who cares about schools, art movements, politics? Each human being—each man and woman— is what interests me!

BREC AS KIPP: Mostly the men...

KAI AS SCHÖNBERG: You are very good at talking both sides of your mouth—is that how you say it in English?

ELLIS AS MAHLER: Who else is culpable? Franz Erlich, another Bauhaus student, who designed the elegant gate at Buchenwald—

OWEN AS GROPIUS: He was imprisoned there as a Communist!

ELLIS AS MAHLER: But the lettering—so beautiful, so Bauhaus—*jedem das seine*—

DUCK AS REMEDIOS: What does that mean?

OWEN AS GROPIUS: "To each his own."

KAI AS SCHÖNBERG: "You get what you deserve."

ELLIS AS MAHLER: Hitler closed the school, but that doesn't make the students saints and martyrs. Always you cannot say "I was just the designer."

OWEN AS GROPIUS: The Nazis wanted Kandinsky fired, and instead Mies closed the school.

ELLIS AS MAHLER: *(To* KAI AS SCHÖNBERG*)* Your old friend Kandinsky.

KAI AS SCHÖNBERG: We never spoke from 1925 until he died seven years ago.

OWEN AS GROPIUS: *(To* BREC AS KIPP*)* You invited her to torture us?

BREC AS KIPP: *(Horrified)* No!

OWEN AS GROPIUS: Because I rescinded your admission to the Bauhaus?

BREC AS KIPP: I only wanted you all to see each other.

ELLIS AS MAHLER: And your *schmatas*!

KAI AS SCHÖNBERG: May I have more champagne?

*(*DUCK AS REMEDIOS *looks to* BREC AS KIPP, *who nods almost imperceptibly.)*

ELLIS AS MAHLER: Me, too!

*(*DUCK AS REMEDIOS *pours* KAI AS SCHÖNBERG *half a glass.)*

KAI AS SCHÖNBERG: Fill it, please.

*(*DUCK AS REMEDIOS *fills the glass and* KAI AS SCHÖNBERG *downs it instantly.)*

BREC AS KIPP: I don't usually show my looms, very secret, but perhaps you'd like to see—

KAI AS SCHÖNBERG: Now. Now I have had enough champagne!

ELLIS AS MAHLER: *Señor, por favor!*

KAI AS SCHÖNBERG: *Nein!*

(DUCK AS REMEDIOS *moves the bottle away from* ELLIS AS MAHLER.)

OWEN AS GROPIUS: Alma, you've had more than your share.

ELLIS AS MAHLER: I have not! This is hospitality, Frau Kipp?

KAI AS SCHÖNBERG: I will give you your share. You ruined my friendship with the great Kandinsky, and now you've poisoned my relationship with Thomas Mann—

ELLIS AS MAHLER: You tried to steal the rights to his *Faustus!*

KAI AS SCHÖNBERG: What an aggravating woman! Gropius, how did you stand it? She cuckolded you with every artist—

ELLIS AS MAHLER: And composer!

(*Silence for a moment, except for the sounds of the drips from the ceiling falling in the buckets.*)

(ELLIS AS MAHLER *off* SCHÖNBERG'*s stricken look:*)

ELLIS AS MAHLER: Yes, Gropius knows, Schönberg.

OWEN AS GROPIUS: I did not know for sure actually until now.

KAI AS SCHÖNBERG: Did you know she also tried to seduce Kandinsky—?

OWEN AS GROPIUS: Kandinsky? Perhaps.

ELLIS AS MAHLER: I did not!

KAI AS SCHÖNBERG: But Kandinsky rejected her.

KAI AS SCHÖNBERG: Which is why she told me he made anti-Semitic remarks!

ELLIS AS MAHLER: He did not!

ELLIS AS MAHLER: He did, too!

KAI AS SCHÖNBERG: To kill our friendship!

OWEN AS GROPIUS: That I have wondered about for 30 years.

ELLIS AS MAHLER: Kandinsky *was* an anti-Semite!

KAI AS SCHÖNBERG: And so are you, you abominable creature!

ELLIS AS MAHLER: That didn't stop you putting your *Yiddishe Mund auf mein Muschi*! [mouth on my cunt]

(*Again silence. Maybe the drips are faster or louder.*)

KAI AS SCHÖNBERG: And now another friendship have you destroyed! You make me want to—ach, this goddamn dripping—you make me to—urinate!

(KAI AS SCHÖNBERG *runs off. Everyone just stares at* ELLIS AS MAHLER. *She shrugs.*)

OWEN AS GROPIUS: Frau Kipp, I can see you've done very well in America even without the Bauhaus degree. Congratulations.

ELLIS AS MAHLER: Yes, professional success, for women so elusive.

BREC AS KIPP: You're too kind.

ELLIS AS MAHLER: You're a phenomenon.

OWEN AS GROPIUS: If you invited Alma here out of malice, God has punished you— (*Holds out his hand to catch a drip)* —As much as the rest of us for your mistake.

ELLIS AS MAHLER: I am her mistake?

OWEN AS GROPIUS: Alma, darling, you were everyone's mistake. Now you are a seventy-two year old woman—

ELLIS AS MAHLER: I'm in my late—fifties—

OWEN AS GROPIUS: You can no longer mesmerize with your body, so you scandalize with your tongue.

(Although extremely drunk, ELLIS AS MAHLER *conjures dignity with a change of posture, sticks out her tongue at* OWEN AS GROPIUS, *and disappears.)*

BREC AS KIPP: You gentlemen are ganging up on a poor widow.

*(*OWEN AS GROPIUS *snorts.)*

BREC AS KIPP: I will understand if you wish to leave, Herr Gropius.

DUCK AS REMEDIOS: But there's a little champagne left, and many samples to see.

OWEN AS GROPIUS: I'm not quite ready to leave.

*(*DUCK AS REMEDIOS *pours. They all start to sit,* OWEN AS GROPIUS *alighting momentarily in a Wassily chair but quickly moving to the Barcelona chair.)*

OWEN AS GROPIUS: I feel a vague responsibility toward the two elderly Teutons who've disappeared in your studio. And I admire your fabrics, I see Bauhaus in every thread.

BREC AS KIPP: *(Showing a sample)* I've experimented recently with more and more metallics—

(Lights out on them and up on KAI AS SCHÖNBERG *trying to urinate in a toilet. Outside the bathroom door stands* ELLIS AS MAHLER.)*

ELLIS AS MAHLER: Schönberg, what are you doing in there?

KAI AS SCHÖNBERG: Driddling!

ELLIS AS MAHLER: I don't hear the music of your tinkle tinkle.

KAI AS SCHÖNBERG: I am seventy-six! Leave me in peace and I will finish faster.

ELLIS AS MAHLER: I need to use the toilet, too.

KAI AS SCHÖNBERG: Squat in the alley.

ELLIS AS MAHLER: It's not urgent. We can have a little tête-a-tête through the door. Although I guess that would be a tête-a-porte-a-tête.

KAI AS SCHÖNBERG: We have embarrassed ourselves already in front of your husband—

ELLIS AS MAHLER: Ex-husband! (*She begins removing her clothes.*)

KAI AS SCHÖNBERG: —And Frau Kipp—

ELLIS AS MAHLER: And her Latin lover.

KAI AS SCHÖNBERG: You are a dirty-minded whore.

ELLIS AS MAHLER: Is that your memory of me, darling? Not my wit, my skin, my sparkling eyes—

KAI AS SCHÖNBERG: You were beautiful once, we all admit it, to our shame.

ELLIS AS MAHLER: Or my music? Do you remember this: (*Hums a tune*)

KAI AS SCHÖNBERG: That's Zemlinsky!

ELLIS AS MAHLER: Or this? (*Hums another tune*)

KAI AS SCHÖNBERG: That's Mahler!

ELLIS AS MAHLER: Where do you think he got it?

KAI AS SCHÖNBERG: Being dead, Mahler can't defend himself.

ELLIS AS MAHLER: Mahler adored me! You did, too.

KAI AS SCHÖNBERG: It was lust only.

ELLIS AS MAHLER: A ripe young girl—

KAI AS SCHÖNBERG: You were over forty, I am sure.

ELLIS AS MAHLER: But what a body still I had in those days!

KAI AS SCHÖNBERG: You are making it difficult to pee.

ELLIS AS MAHLER: I have that effect on men.

(ELLIS AS MAHLER *is almost fully disrobed by now and has a beautiful young body [which may be male or female, depending on casting].)*

KAI AS SCHÖNBERG: *Mein Gott!*

ELLIS AS MAHLER: Such sacred memories! With just a stroke of my little finger I persuaded you to leave that Bauhaus party in 1920—

KAI AS SCHÖNBERG: A party to my honor!

ELLIS AS MAHLER: But you left the party to make love to me on Gropius' flat roof. Maybe we caused those leaks!

KAI AS SCHÖNBERG: Never am I going to piss!

ELLIS AS MAHLER: When you come out of there, Schönberg, I want you to see me in 1920, see me with the eyes of memory.

KAI AS SCHÖNBERG: I won't look at you one second! Have you no feeling for Getrud?

ELLIS AS MAHLER: Your wife's not here. I am. You are.

KAI AS SCHÖNBERG: We are in Mrs Kipp's weaving studio!

(KAI AS SCHÖNBERG *bursts out of the WC and sees* ELLIS AS MAHLER *displayed before him completely nude. For a moment he is stupified.*)

ELLIS AS MAHLER: The eyes of memory…!

OWEN AS GROPIUS: *(From the darkness)* Beautiful.

KAI AS SCHÖNBERG: Alma, full always of surprises.

(Lights out on them and up on OWEN AS GROPIUS, BREC AS KIPP *and* DUCK AS REMEDIOS. OWEN AS GROPIUS *examines a particular sample.)*

OWEN AS GROPIUS: Very beautiful indeed.

BREC AS KIPP: Have you been to Bullocks Wilshire?

OWEN AS GROPIUS: The department store?

DUCK AS REMEDIOS: Seven blocks directly south—

BREC AS KIPP: You might be familiar with the interior designer. Jock Peters. Originally Jacob Detlof.

OWEN AS GROPIUS: Oh! He worked for Peter Behrens. He changed his name?

BREC AS KIPP: *(Nods)* He designed the interiors of Bullocks Wilshire when it opened in 1928 and used my draperies in the tea rooms.

OWEN AS GROPIUS: Is this thread synthetic?

BREC AS KIPP: Lurex.

OWEN AS GROPIUS: Otti Berger patented some patterns with metallic yarns.

BREC AS KIPP: I never met her.

OWEN AS GROPIUS: Yours only bears a passing resemblance to Otti's—it's impressive— *(Chokes up)* I apologize—

BREC AS KIPP:	DUCK AS REMEDIOS:
Director Gropius—!	Some water? More champagne?

OWEN AS GROPIUS: *(Accepting champagne)* Only today did I realize Otti died in a concentration camp designed by Fritz Ertl. Made efficient and artistic by his time at our school!

BREC AS KIPP:
Design is neither moral
nor immoral—

DUCK AS REMEDIOS:
You couldn't predict—

OWEN AS GROPIUS: When we founded the Bauhaus in 1919 our manifesto was deeply moral—design for the people. But it can be perverted—my own motto "art and technology, a new unity" was twisted by the corporations funding the New Bauhaus in Chicago, which is why it didn't work—!

(KAI AS SCHÖNBERG *appears, perhaps out of breath.*)

OWEN AS GROPIUS: Arnold, I am sorry.

KAI AS SCHÖNBERG: No, I must apologize—what happened with me and Alma—

OWEN AS GROPIUS: She did the same with me while married to Mahler.

KAI AS SCHÖNBERG: She is no longer your responsibility—

OWEN AS GROPIUS: This rotten world doesn't revolve around Alma. I am sorry for being German. For your brother killed by the Nazis—

KAI AS SCHÖNBERG: You know of that?

OWEN AS GROPIUS: How could I not know it? I am German. Being in America does not excuse me.

KAI AS SCHÖNBERG: Walter, you were forced out as we all were.

OWEN AS GROPIUS: I could have stayed. I wouldn't have ended up in Buchenwald.

DUCK AS REMEDIOS: Have you ever been to a concentration camp?

OWEN AS GROPIUS: No!

BREC AS KIPP:	KAI AS SCHÖNBERG:
Zeno!	I couldn't bear it!

OWEN AS GROPIUS: Have you?

DUCK AS REMEDIOS: Dachau. Our division was the first to arrive.

BREC AS KIPP: Please do not tell us about it. We've seen the newsreels.

OWEN AS GROPIUS: I would like to hear.

KAI AS SCHÖNBERG: From an American.

DUCK AS REMEDIOS: May I, Mrs Kipp?

BREC AS KIPP: Very well, but we are all rather sick of it.

DUCK AS REMEDIOS: I will only say it changed me. We Americans—seeing such horror—the starving inmates, the smoke and the smell—

BREC AS KIPP: Oh! Please!

DUCK AS REMEDIOS: We soldiers didn't all behave… as we should. The shame of the place stuck to us. So I understand, Director Gropius, how you feel sorry to be German. Sometimes I feel sorry to be American.

OWEN AS GROPIUS:	BREC AS KIPP:
America is wonderful!	Zeno, how can you say that?

KAI AS SCHÖNBERG: American soldiers were our heroes! You were!

DUCK AS REMEDIOS: We had concentration camps, too.

BREC AS KIPP:	OWEN AS GROPIUS:
That's not what they were!	American concentration camps?

BREC AS KIPP: Relocation camps for the Japanese.

KAI AS SCHÖNBERG: I remember. Right here in California.

DUCK AS REMEDIOS: I loved a woman who spent two years in one of those camps.

BREC AS KIPP: Zeno, how horrible. I'm so sorry.

KAI AS SCHÖNBERG: But she wasn't killed, systematically exterm—

DUCK AS REMEDIOS: No, the war ended.

KAI AS SCHÖNBERG: Only the Germans—

DUCK AS REMEDIOS: She and I visited Manzanar together so we could both understand. We stopped seeing each other soon after. I think it's because we reminded each other of the past.

KAI AS SCHÖNBERG: The past is important! History is important.

OWEN AS GROPIUS: Dachau opened the year the Bauhaus closed.

(ELLIS AS MAHLER *appears fully clothed but tangled in a mess of threads.*)

DUCK AS REMEDIOS:
Mrs Werfel!

BREC AS KIPP:
Gott in Himmel!

OWEN AS GROPIUS:
Alma, what have you done?

KAI AS SCHÖNBERG:
Wretched creature!

ELLIS AS MAHLER: What intricate looms, Frau Kipp. I found myself quite drawn to them, pulled in by the beauty of your designs— *(Pulling threads off)* —So modern, so sleek, so Bauhaus—

BREC AS KIPP: *(Running past* ELLIS AS MAHLER*) Wenn du sie kaputt hast*—! [If you've broken them—!]

OWEN AS GROPIUS: You are so jealous of her success?

KAI AS SCHÖNBERG: More champagne, please!

DUCK AS REMEDIOS: Excuse me a moment!

(DUCK AS REMEDIOS *disappears after* BREC AS KIPP. KAI AS SCHÖNBERG *can't find his glass and drinks right from the bottle.*)

OWEN AS GROPIUS: You are all the forces against the Bauhaus arrayed, the conservative government of Thuringia, the Nazis on the Dessau town council, Hitler himself declaring art degenerate—you are the worst of Germany, our most monstrous export—!

ELLIS AS MAHLER: I am American now.

OWEN AS GROPIUS: If I had known you were coming—

ELLIS AS MAHLER: You would have dressed better.

OWEN AS GROPIUS: Because of Schönberg I came, but left almost when I saw you.

ELLIS AS MAHLER: And yet you stay. Help me with this, would you, darling?

(*Reluctantly,* OWEN AS GROPIUS *picks threads from her. She tosses them, he handles them almost reverently.* KAI AS SCHÖNBERG *keeps drinking from the bottle.*)

OWEN AS GROPIUS: I stay because I need to apologize to Frau Kipp. We've all done shameful things—

KAI AS SCHÖNBERG:	OWEN AS GROPIUS:
Some more than others!	—On our way to America, and we didn't leave all of our mess behind in Europe.

OWEN AS GROPIUS: I committed a great error against Frau Kipp—

ELLIS AS MAHLER: You slept with her?

OWEN AS GROPIUS: No, did you?

(KAI AS SCHÖNBERG *snorts his champagne.*)

Owen as Gropius: I used her in my war with Itten—

Kai as Schönberg: Ellis as Mahler:
Did you provoke that one,   You treated Itten
too, Alma?   shamefully as well.

Owen as Gropius: Yes, yes, I did.

Kai as Schönberg: Did you *schtup* also Itten, Alma? (*She rolls her eyes. Of course she did.*)

Owen as Gropius: At this age one does not give up so much by saying sorry. You must to Frau Kipp apologize as well, for destroying her design—

(Brec as Kipp *entering with* Duck as Remedios*:*)

Brec as Kipp: She destroyed more than that— (*Displays some wooden parts*) —She broke my loom!

Ellis as Mahler: It was an accident. I fell. If you are lucky I will not sue.

Brec as Kipp: I am sorry, but I must ask you to leave.

Owen as Gropius: Frau Kipp, I apologize—

Brec as Kipp: She is not your fault! She is mine for inviting her.

Owen as Gropius: I apologize for not accepting you into the Bauhaus. I criticize myself very sharp. The Bauhaus is alive in you—in these threads—eighteen years after it shut down.

Brec as Kipp: That…is so much more than I expected.

Owen as Gropius: And this I like very much. (*Shows sample*) Would you be willing to contract with General Panel Corporation for all our draperies?

Ellis as Mahler: Gropius, so susceptible.

Owen as Gropius: To beauty, yes, I admit it.

Brec as Kipp: I don't know what to say.

DUCK AS REMEDIOS: Say thank you! Thank you very much! *Danke schön! Gracias!*

OWEN AS GROPIUS: And for the loom I will compensate you.

KAI AS SCHÖNBERG: Gropius, you'll do no such thing! Alma can afford to pay it—

BREC AS KIPP: That is very generous, Herr Director, but not necessary—

ELLIS AS MAHLER: I can't! Werfel left me with debts only!

KAI AS SCHÖNBERG: So that is it? You're looking for your fourth husband? And so desperate you go back thirty years to find him?

ELLIS AS MAHLER: Not thirty years. Fifteen minutes ago you had your hand on me in the toilet.

KAI AS SCHÖNBERG: When I pushed you aside as you blocked my way with your gray-spotted naked body, displaying yourself like a prostitute's cadaver!

DUCK AS REMEDIOS: We're all out of champagne. Would anyone like water?

BREC AS KIPP: Or coffee?

ELLIS AS MAHLER: I am not so old as you, Schönberg.

OWEN AS GROPIUS: She is seventy-two. She showed herself naked?

BREC AS KIPP: In our toilet?

ELLIS AS MAHLER: You are four years older than I.

OWEN AS GROPIUS: And I'm four years younger than you, Alma. What is the point of mentioning it?

ELLIS AS MAHLER: Frau Kipp, do you remember the Buahaus party in honor of Schönberg?

<table>
<tr><td>Kai as Schönberg:
I appreciated the party
very much.</td><td>Brec as Kipp:
It was quite nice.</td></tr>
</table>

Ellis as Mahler: But ended badly I recall.

Owen as Gropius: I am astonished you remember a party from thirty years ago. We had parties weekly at the Bauhaus. We celebrated everything.

Ellis as Mahler: But you ruint the party with your terror-stricken outburst, so embarrassing.

<table>
<tr><td>Kai as Schönberg:
What outburst?</td><td>Owen as Gropius:
I don't remember any
outburst.</td></tr>
</table>

Ellis as Mahler: Thirteen.

<table>
<tr><td>Owen as Gropius:
What?</td><td>Brec as Kipp:
Oh.</td></tr>
</table>

Kai as Schönberg: I don't know what—

Ellis as Mahler: Frau Kipp remembers. Schönberg practically suffered a stroke when someone mentioned the number thirteen. Isn't that so, Frau Kipp?

Brec as Kipp: Perhaps.

Ellis as Mahler: I noticed it even now when I said the word. Schönberg blanched when I said thirteen.

Kai as Schönberg: You will be happy to know my fear I have conquered of the number.

Ellis as Mahler: Which number?

Owen as Gropius: Alma, enough.

Ellis as Mahler: If you have conquered it, you can say it, surely.

Kai as Schönberg: *(After some effort)* Thirteen. See? I am over it, but the fear was quite debilitating. I even sought the advice of a psychic, was terrified of 1939 because it's a multiple—

ELLIS AS MAHLER: Three times thirteen.

KAI AS SCHÖNBERG: But I survived!

BREC AS KIPP: I believe it's stopped raining.

ELLIS AS MAHLER: Four times thirteen is fifty-two—next year.

DUCK AS REMEDIOS: *(Collecting buckets)* I'll take these out.

KAI AS SCHÖNBERG: I've outlived that superstition.

ELLIS AS MAHLER: *(Pointedly)* You're seventy-six.

DUCK AS REMEDIOS:	BREC AS KIPP:
You look very well for seventy-six, Herr Schönberg.	Oh, no—!

ELLIS AS MAHLER: How funny! I just realized: seven and six add up to thirteen!

(KAI AS SCHÖNBERG *gasps.*)

ELLIS AS MAHLER: And today is Friday the thirteenth!

OWEN AS GROPIUS: Alma, I'm taking you home!

ELLIS AS MAHLER:	KAI AS SCHÖNBERG:
I thought you'd never ask!	Seventy-six! I never thought—

BREC AS KIPP: It doesn't mean anything, Herr Schönberg—

ELLIS AS MAHLER: It does to him!

KAI AS SCHÖNBERG: Seventy-six on Friday the thirteenth!

OWEN AS GROPIUS: Arnold, I'll take you home. Alma can stay here and rot!

BREC AS KIPP:	ELLIS AS MAHLER:
You can't leave her here!	*(Grabbing* DUCK AS

REMEDIOS*)* I'll stay here
with Señor Remedios!

DUCK AS REMEDIOS:
(Wriggling away)
Excuse me, Mrs Werfel!

KAI AS SCHÖNBERG:
I knew it! I knew it!

*(*KAI AS SCHÖNBERG *heads toward the door but stumbles over the buckets.)*

BREC AS KIPP:
Herr Schönberg, be
careful!

OWEN AS GROPIUS:
Be logical!

OWEN AS GROPIUS: Nothing happened when you turned sixty-seven!

DUCK AS REMEDIOS: Or fifty-eight!

BREC AS KIPP:
Or forty-nine!

KAI AS SCHÖNBERG:
All my life, I knew it!

(Knocking buckets all over, KAI AS SCHÖNBERG *stumbles into the audience.)*

KAI AS SCHÖNBERG: You can't create, so you destroy, absorb enough to find the weakness then suck the life out of everything, everyone! *(As he falls into the audience)* Goddamn you, Alma! *(Silence for a moment. He just lies there.)*

ELLIS AS MAHLER: *(To the audience)* And thus the great Arnold Schönberg died with my name on his lips.

BREC AS KIPP: He isn't dead.

ELLIS AS MAHLER: He just broke the fourth wall and fell into the audience. That's the end.

OWEN AS GROPIUS: Actually, Arnold Schönberg died later that night. *(Transforms into* OWEN, *English accent)* Fifteen minutes before midnight on Friday, July 13, 1951.

BREC AS KIPP: In his own bed— *(Transforms into* BREC, *California accent, hands on hips)* —With his wife Gertrud by his side.

*(*ELLIS AS MAHLER *shrugs.)*

BREC: Maria Kipp's new studio was a huge success, with commissions from Walt Disney, Frank Sinatra, Dinah Shore, Max Factor, Ricardo Montalban, Bob Hope and Rita Hayworth. She designed the original drapes for LACMA and the first upholstery for Air Force One. Maria Kipp died in 1988.

OWEN: General Panel Corporation went out of business later that year, but the flat-roofed house the company built in Nichols Canyon survives to this day. The roof was replaced most recently in 2006. Walter Gropius retired from Harvard in 1952, won the Goethe Prize in 1961 and died in Boston in 1969.

ELLIS AS MAHLER: Alma Schindler Mahler Gropius Werfel left Los Angeles for New York in 1952— *(Becomes* ELLIS, *Southern accent)* —Where she published two—

ALL: Heavily fictionalized!

ELLIS: —Autobiographies in 1958 in English and in 1960 in German. She died in 1964 and was buried in Vienna near Gustav Mahler and Manon Gropius, so they wouldn't miss her funeral.

DUCK AS REMEDIOS: Zenobio Remedios did not die— *(Becomes* DUCK*)* Because he is fictional character.

KAI: *(Rising, no longer* SCHÖNBERG*)* Just as the Bauhaus never died.

BREC: Shut down three times—

DUCK: By government!

BREC: It always resurrected.

KAI: The German diaspora—

BREC: The Jewish diaspora—   KAI: —Before, during and after the war—

KAI: —Spread the Bauhaus idea throughout the world.

DUCK: But mostly to United States.

OWEN: Immigrants with ideas.

BREC: And in 1967 Berlin and Los Angeles became Sister Cities..

(They fill their champagne glasses.)

OWEN: We hope you enjoyed our presentation, the third and final in the Bauhaus series, not only because the Bauhaus history is complete, but also because—

(They all produce green envelopes.)

ELLIS: We're graduating, y'all!

BREC: All of us!

DUCK: *(Bursting out)* I go to grad school for composition!

KAI: Hence the screaming? OWEN: Thornton School of Music!

KAI: *(Cynically)* At USC.

DUCK: Base on music from Bauhaus presentation. I just find out! Student visa extended!

ELLIS: I just have to say—

EVERYONE ELSE: No, you don't!

ELLIS: —That when we started this assignment, I never even heard of the Bauhaus. I thought history was boring—

KAI: I thought it was irrelevant.

DUCK: I no hear of Holocaust.

BREC: History is the shit!

ELLIS: History gave the world the idea of you.

(Everyone looks either confused, skeptical or at the floor.)

ELLIS: You know, idea, like the Bauhaus idea!

KAI: With all due respect—

ELLIS: With all due respect, fuck you!

(OWEN puts a gentle hand on ELLIS, and tries to save the situation, which ELLIS silently acknowledges with gratitude.)

OWEN: Good ideas never die.

DUCK: Such like collaboration, cooperation— *(Pronouncing it perfectly)* —Gesamtkunstwerk! Thank you, beloved professor, for assignment that force us collaborate.

BREC: *(As they toast)* To elegant, affordable design—

DUCK: —For the people!   OWEN: Beauty in utility—

ELLIS: Art and technology. *(Asking permission of audience member who is texting)* May I? *(Takes the phone, shows it)* Bauhaus!

DUCK: *(Borrowing a purse from an audience member)* Bauhaus!

(Projection: a montage of Bauhaus-influenced American and world-wide designs is projected, including universalist fonts, Knoll furniture, International style buildings, the John Hancock Center, MoMA and the Met Breuer. Celebratory music in a Bauhaus style rises in triumph as DUCK, OWEN, KAI and BREC borrow objects from audience members or find them hidden among the seats. The final objects may be ridiculously out of context in a theatre audience, such as a Braun juicer or a Lightolier lamp. They display them as they speak:)

KAI: Bauhaus!

BREC: Bauhaus!

OWEN: Bauhaus!

ELLIS: Bauhaus!

DUCK: Or as we say here in America:

ALL: Ikea!

END OF PLAY

(As the audience exits the theatre, they may notice that the rhyparography sculpture has been sold [perhaps simply a red dot on the wall next to the object label]. The actor playing KAI *may be standing by proudly.)*